Praise for Book of Potions

"Potion: That which, when swallowed, has the power to change the world around us. In this marvelous collection, Lauren K. Watel has profoundly altered my sense of what a poem can do and be. The land-and heart-scapes she conjures into being are both strange and uncannily familiar. Here is a poet who shows no mercy to the usual consolations of sentiment. I have not read so brilliant, so transformative and technically masterful a book of poems in years."

—Linda Gregerson, author of *Canopy*

"Lauren K. Watel's *Book of Potions* comprises parables, gnostic and enigmatic narrative arcs and loops, secret recipes for the imagination, incantatory dramas, fierce judgments of the mind, equally fierce compassions, and a constant adventure of reflection that reflects not just the human self but the entire inner and outer dreamscape in which the self abides. A flawlessly written book of poems, powerful and self-contained in its sounds and its silences."

—Vijay Seshadri, author of *That Was Now, This Is Then*

"When Kafka, writing his parables and fables, died, his gift transmigrated, with all its sly and despairing invention, its pitch-perfect ironies and imagistic and associative waywardness, into the soul of Lauren K. Watel. Her prose poems are the best kind of prose and the best kind of poem: offbeat, now fierce, now funny, acutely attuned to her own life and the life we live now: war, suicide, manias of all kinds; an ever-expanding sense of dread and of lost possibility; love always on the brink of fulfillment colliding with human limitation; but never dour or preachy or easy to pin down. Her syntactic brilliance captures every least nuance of the personal, the social, and the spiritual."   —Tom Sleigh, author of *The King's Touch*

"*Book of Potions* is a collection evoking the nineteenth century and early Modernist poetic innovations that created the prose poem, akin to the work of Charles Baudelaire, Francis Ponge, and Samuel Beckett in ironic edginess and the wandering itineraries of unconsoled dreams. Yet I also see kinship in the Chinese poets of the T'ang who wrote mysterious, metaphysical dream-prose about journeys into other worlds—like the Taoist mondo of Chuang-tzu who dreamed he was a butterfly, then wrote he might've been a butterfly dreaming he was a man. In the way of these literary ancestors, Watel's own prose is cadenced, composed, and plotted as much by sound as the sense of dreams. Its style is refined, beautifully lyric, mysterious, and emerges from the heightened imagination of poetic flight. Nothing in American verse is quite like it. It is the poetry of the universe of ten thousand things."   —Garrett Hongo, author of *Coral Road*

"After drinking these potions Lauren K. Watel has brewed, I am at least one hundred years wiser. I wish I knew what spoon she used to stir poetry into prose with such mastery, such tenderness. Believe me when I tell you, I swallowed this book whole and grew a second heart."
                    —Sabrina Orah Mark, author of *Happily*

"Just under the surface of Lauren K. Watel's sassy, wry, quizzical prose poems, nightmares thrum. Masks slip, and faces are missing; armies march; the speaker is 'playing solitaire at the end of the world'; recurrently, a father shoots himself in the head. Watel converts mayhem to fable, and makes a style out of survival. A gallant and original book."   —Rosanna Warren, author of *So Forth*

"The playfully resonant title of Lauren K. Watel's *Book of Potions* not only positions it between genres, but also signals a book in a constant, fluid state of betweenness: a book fluxing between dream and awakening, between present, past, and future, illusion and disillusion. Each tightly composed 'potion' has the completeness of a prose poem, but each page turned is also a transition, a jump cut, another inventive link in an interior narration of ongoing transformation. Watel's style is a powerful element of her voice. There's wit, chiseled sentences, vivid imagery, and given the interiority, the presiding effect, rather than cinematic, is kinetic. *Book of Potions* is a masterpiece of sustained prose rhythm, and a wonderfully original debut."

—Stuart Dybek, author of *Streets in Their Own Ink*

"Lauren K. Watel resituates language in these precise, startling, and mordant prose poems. Attuned to the times and to all time, the author stewards these gorgeous pieces with a fine-tuned sense of how best to enter a reader's heart and mind."

—Amy Hempel, author of *Sing to It*

BOOK

of

POTIONS

poems

LAUREN *k.* WATEL

Sarabande Books ◉ *Louisville, Kentucky*

Publisher's Cataloging-In-Publication Data
(Provided by Cassidy Cataloguing Services, Inc.).

Names: Watel, Lauren K., author.
Title:Book of potions : poems / Lauren K. Watel.
Description: First edition. | Louisville, Kentucky : Sarabande Books, [2025]
Identifiers: ISBN: 978-1-956046-35-9 (paperback) | 978-1-956046-36-6 (ebook)
Subjects: LCSH: Middle-aged women--Poetry. | Social norms--Poetry. | Sex role--Poetry. |
Stereotypes (Social psychology)--Poetry. | Feminism--Poetry. | LCGFT: Prose poems.
Classification: LCC: PS3623.A86836 B66 2025 | DDC: 811/.6--dc23

Cover and interior by Danika Isdahl.

Printed in USA.
This book is printed on acid-free paper.
Sarabande Books is a nonprofit literary organization.

This project is supported in part by an award from the National Endowment for the Arts. The Kentucky Arts Council, the state arts agency, supports Sarabande Books with state tax dollars and federal funding from the National Endowment for the Arts.

This book is for Louis,
whose goodness makes so many futures possible

CONTENTS

NO INTRODUCTION NEEDED

IN *the* WHITE ROOM

NIGHTFALL

ENJOY the MAYHEM

GO BY, GO BY

AMERICAN DREAMSCAPES:
ON LAUREN K. WATEL'S BOOK *of* POTIONS

If in a thousand years an archeologist finds this collection, they might not know anything about our empire, its wars, American daily life, but they will learn quite a bit about our psyche, which is to say our dreamscapes. It is as if with this book of dreams—anxious, tender, angry, longing, funny, stand-offish, lyrical, incantatory, haunting, nightmarish—Lauren K. Watel has given us a kind of X-ray of our time, our country (with its horrific gun violence and its pretty suburban kitchens), its pulse.

Now, let me be clear, this isn't something that the reader might think right away, as they open *Book of Potions*. I didn't, for sure, but as I turned the pages, this realization grew, and it became unstoppable. At first I marveled at the imagination, its reach. Here is a taste: "Out in the country the tree comes alight every night with fireflies, and the sky glows a cool blue, like a painting of loneliness, and the birds fly in from days gone by. They land in the branches of the evening, singing of their darkening business."

Then I found myself falling for the tonal shifts, for how tonally alive these pages are, their humor. Listen to this: "Meanwhile an angel appeared. A man angel, all clean-shaven and smelling of cigarettes, and he was wearing white robes, like angels do in movies. He seemed none too pleased about it, having to wear white robes. . . . But there he was, on the corner of Stanton and Ludlow in his white robes and gleaming chin."

This humor goes hand in hand with irony, of course. But the difference between Watel and many of her contemporaries is the fact that her irony always contains a metaphysical element. In short, she might have the angst of a *Seinfeld* character, but the dark, soul-level torment of Gogol is not far behind. I wondered how one could live on a daily basis with that kind of biting metaphysical irony and get away with it. This is a relentless, bracingly honest accounting, with the occasional reprieve of jubilation: "when chords started up from the guitar, crashing through that battered amp, song that sounded like an uprising, loud and strident and brash, I could have died of it, the joy."

What unites a collection comprising such different visions is the formidable uniformity of the speaker's voice. Watel's voice is unmistakably hers—driven, energetic, rhythmical, lyrical. It is a voice whose timbre also serves as a kind of self-portrait, for every image here is charged with tone, and its many self-revelations: "My hair, my skin, a map of experiments . . . over a half century of wandering these sidewalks."

As I turned the pages, I found myself more and more impressed at how revealing these dreams are, though in no way confessional. One *gets* the person behind the page, without needing the biography. Here, a dream might often be a psychological portrait, or in reverse, a psychological portrait that might be a dream: "I was at the gallery alone. Now I saw it was because all my friends were there, in frames. No wonder they weren't available when I called to invite them to the opening."

As the book went on, I began to wonder: how is she going to pull it off, having so many pieces in the same form? Yes, the nerve of this book is formidable. "Go on the nerve alone," Frank O'Hara once suggested to us. Yes, imagination here is impressive, too. I think Borges might have found himself enjoying these pages quite a bit. Yes, I loved the idea of a potion, which suggests an invention of form specifically for this very content, and a hybrid vision naturally requests a hybrid delivery.

But how will the book sustain so much *uniformity* in its form, I wondered. Instead of giving in, Watel doubles down. Repetitions begin—and this is a brilliant move on her part, as what starts as a formal project becomes literally haunting. Thus, the incantations of "What Sounds"—as the title reappears through the book—haunts our auditory organ, expanding our idea of what sounds, resounding, resonant, echoing, can be. We learn on one page that "what sounds like rain is tires on asphalt. What sounds like sunlight is death in the trees." And some pages later: "What sounds like music is the insect approach of twilight." And, further on: "What sounds like silence is anger. Look, over there, it's your father and grandfather and their fathers and grandfathers and so on, lining up, arms akimbo, across a field."

The repetitions of "In the White Room" deliver a striking punch. The question at the heart of these poems is, appropriately: "Where is everyone?" Food for thought in a book so *crowded* with everyone. As white rooms keep popping up, they bring this question into focus, and in the final white room we find this: "My hands clutch this notebook as if it were the hand of my father, dying of a self-inflicted gunshot wound to the head. He was in a white room of his own. Or was it night in there? Hard to tell." This is where one realizes—and cannot escape this realization—that the white rooms of mental illness and gun violence haunt this sequence.

The imaginative scope and range of *Book of Potions* is marvelous. With so much tonal invention and play, not to mention grief, solitude, tenderness, angst and bravery, the book is truly a dreamscape: Watel has built a house with myriad rooms, each of them a dream that keeps spiraling. There is something reminiscent of Kafka's parables in Watel's perspective, something Calvinoesque and Borgesian and even Gogolian, yes. But in the end, I felt, the book has a peculiarly American metaphysics of the self, an isolated and estranged self constantly grappling with the larger forces. Out of this metaphysics a human voice begins to speak, and through speaking rearranges the landscape as we know it.

—Ilya Kaminsky

BOOK *of* POTIONS

potion = poem + fiction

NO INTRODUCTION NEEDED

I AWOKE ON THE EDGE

I awoke on the edge of a field, a snow-covered meadow plated with sunlight, and the sky was bright white and unnatural, and the silence was white, too, a ravenous silence, and the birds had all gone away, and the squirrels were burrowed in the deep, and behind me the trees creaked in their bones, and the snow clung to their limbs, to their limbs down to the needles, the snow was layers thick and smooth, flawless across its surface like something spread by a machine, and sunlight skimmed over the snow as if it were an impenetrable metal, and I stepped onto the field holding my breath because I didn't know how firm the snow was, or how deep, but it wasn't the snow that gave with my every step, it was the silence, how I sank into it up to my knees, the silence crackling around my feet, pulling me down with a sharp gravity, and I slogged through the silence, my breath shrouding my face, and the silence sliced through my lips, through my throat and into my lungs, the silence swallowed up my chest, and how close it seemed, the other side, so I kept going, kept stepping across the snow-covered meadow, across the sunlight, across the glittering silence, which lit me up, me, who'd always bristled in silence, darkly.

THEY BROUGHT HER IN

They brought her in to sit in the audience. They brought her in to listen. They brought her in to look pretty and keep her mouth shut. They brought her in to laugh at the right times. They brought her in to pour the wine and eat the crumbs. Do they want her opinion? Do they want her story? Heavens no, they want her to keep her opinions and stories to herself. Or, better yet, not to have any. How is it they found her in the first place? She isn't listed anywhere. She hasn't joined an agency or put herself on a website, but somehow they found her. They always find her. But why did she say yes, and why did she accept the part? She doesn't know how to act, never did. She's always been too real, too hard to take, a pain in the neck/ass/you-name-it. A headache. When she opens her mouth, something harsh comes out, as if she can't keep the bile down, as if she's been poisoned and she's trying to choke the poison back up, trying to save her very life. And maybe she has. Been poisoned, that is, little by little, sitting in the audience for so long, nodding appreciatively at the monologues, the comic routines, the confessions, looking pretty night after night, trying to keep her mouth shut while laughing at the right times. You've got to hand it to her, she's a good audience. Quite the little listener, as they say. But how can she keep pouring the wine without spilling, and how long can she survive on crumbs?

WHAT'S HAPPENING

What's happening to the tea and the sugar? They're vanishing. The cups are vanishing. Vanishing the saucers, and the table and chairs, into the invisible, the overlight wideness. Where will we sit when the chairs are gone, and where will we eat when the table is gone? Vanishing the parking lots, and the cars with their rusted underbellies. Vanishing the yellow lines, and the road signs. Where will we go and how will we steer when the cars are gone, the trains abandoned along the tracks like empty skins? How now the moon, plucked from the sky like a plum, and how now the stars, fallen to earth like so much glitter, the stars quilting the meadows like a frost, the stars with their lights gone out. How now the sun, as big as the sky itself and a fiery white. And the stars are as ash. And night is as ash, vanishing, and the day so white and broad, pouring into every crevice and corner. Vanishing the secrets and the hiding places. Vanishing all the ever unknowns. The shadows are vanishing, the day saturating the earth, the wide white day, the sun a burning tyranny. The night, all the darknesses, the secrets and the hiding places, these will be memories, and even they will burn, turn pale and thin, fade into the sky, into the light and the bottomless sun. And here we go, we are diving into the white, the wide, windowless white, and it doesn't matter if our eyes are open or shut, everything looks the same, and it doesn't matter if we're naked or clothed, because we can't see ourselves. Vanishing we are, ash we are, as we swim through the white, vanishing our hair, and our nails, vanishing, our vision, all our senses, vanishing into the overlight wideness, the wetlike white, the vanishing, the very vanishing.

NO INTRODUCTION NEEDED

No introduction needed, just state my name. Well, if you insist on a few words, say I'm middle-aged, which you can see for yourself. My hair, my skin, a map of experiments. And as I accomplished very little over a half century of wandering these sidewalks, you can skip my accomplishments and say that I'm tough and mean. Say that I'm harsh, to put the audience at ease, and that as a girl I learned riflery and archery and gymnastics and nature, so I could survive in the wilderness for a day, maybe two. Say that I'm disapproving and critical, qualities I came by honestly, which you'd discover if you met my mother. And susceptible to gloom, to a relentless-yet-useless self-scrutiny, which often devolves to dire universalizing, which often devolves to a down-turning spiral of bleakness from which diminishing chance of escape. Qualities I also came by honestly, which you'd discover if you met my father. Which you won't, because he died years ago in our back driveway, where he installed a basketball hoop one summer. This was after the playhouse and the trampoline and the fort and the bicycle built for two and the mopeds and all the tools rusting on their shelves in the garage, and don't forget the tape and the glue.

WHATEVER YOU DO

Whatever you do, don't open the door. If you hear him knocking, plug up your ears. Keep on going, don't stop, don't open the window, don't answer his call, don't listen to his flattery, don't laugh at his jokes. Keep him out, keep him away. Don't let him on the front porch, don't let him on the back porch. Don't open the gate and let him in the yard. Don't sing his songs. Don't drink the drinks he mixes. Don't eat the apples from his pockets. When he pounds on the door, when he rings the bell, when he writes, waves, howls—ignore him, ignore him. He'll come crawling. He'll come whistling. He'll come telling you what you want to hear. He'll come looking so pretty, a pretty you never thought you'd see, a pretty you can't resist, so don't look, don't even open your eyes. And when he touches your hair, and when he kisses your face, and when he follows you from town to town, bind up your hair or, better yet, cut it off and hide your face, turn it to the sun, erase your tracks and disappear. Because if you answer that door, if you open the window, if you sing his songs, because if you fall for his prettiness and laugh at his jokes, he will steal your very thoughts, and it will be you, only you, who let him in, let him take what wasn't his, and he'll make you feel guilty for calling him a thief.

WHEN I WAS YOUNG

When I was young I had many enemies. I prayed for vengeance night and day, but the gods didn't hear me, and my enemies flourished. As I grew older my desire for vengeance weakened, as did my enemies. By the time I reached old age I no longer sought revenge but craved rest and peace. I died happily, wishing my enemies well.

When I arrived in the lands beyond life, I found that the gods had heard my prayers after all. There were my enemies, every last one, and some I didn't even remember, nor the wrongs they had done me. For each of them the gods had devised a punishment, one more diabolical and torturous than the last, and all of them to the end of time. The screams—they were beyond imagining, and so loud.

THE KINGS

The kings are going blind. The kings are going deaf. The kings are going fat and simple. All day long they eat and drink and sit on their thrones, their joints stiffening. Their subjects smile and flatter them, and the kings believe the flattery, though they should know better. And the queens? Long ago the queens adored the kings, but as the kings saw and heard less and less, the queens saw and heard more and more. Nowadays they walk the castle walls and stare out to sea at the ships approaching from the horizon, the queens ready to leave as soon as the right ship makes harbor. The kings travel their realms and flirt their ways, and the noble daughters smell the power rising off the kings, and the wealth, so they flirt back, because the kings have no heirs. Everyone knows that when the kings die, their dynasties die with them; the queens have no claims and will make none, they want nothing, save to leave, and to forget. Meanwhile the people bide their time. The kings keep losing strength, losing their touch, losing their grip, giving the same speeches, the same winks and squeezes, and the people keep clapping. But they're waiting just the same, for the thrones to sit empty. Any one of them could rule, anyone could take the place of a king, could sit on a throne, because what does it take to rule? Just a crown.

IN THE PORTRAIT GALLERY

In the portrait gallery they were serving champagne. I grabbed a glass from a passing tray and sipped uneasily as I gazed at the portraits. I was at the gallery alone. Now I saw it was because all my friends were there, in frames. No wonder they weren't available when I called to invite them to the opening. Louis was hanging on the wall, as were Jeff and Amber and Rembert. My loved ones also were represented, alive and dead. My son. My parents. My brother and sister. My half brother. My late brother-in-law. My fucked-up would-have-been stepson. Everyone I had gone to school with, Thomas Stuart and Beth and Kerry and Zoë and Sallie and Melinda and Irene and Alex. Even Salah, whose mother taught us French all those years ago. Though unnerved I was somewhat reassured by the size of the show. I thought I had so few friends, but really I'd known a ton of people. And so many of them were attractive and stylish, much to my satisfaction, their features well proportioned, each face a drama of complex expressiveness, a portraitist's dream. But not a one was smiling, up on the wall. They looked overly serious, trapped, as if they'd been captured on the canvas against their will, as if they'd been forced. Which brings me to the fact that I can't remember the painter. The show opened just this evening, but no one seems to know the artist's name, not even the people who work here. What is this gallery, anyway? I've never seen it advertised. It's a nice enough space, if you like cement floors and high windowless walls. But the air, so thin all of a sudden, and the faces so parched and the champagne gone flat, I wish I could find the door.

MARTYRS, ALL OF US

Martyrs, all of us, martyrs to the core. To our causes, saints and martyrs to our gods, to our holy missions, our visions. How sweet they are, how violent, and our wounds, how they bleed. And aren't we beautiful? And don't we glow with a heavenly light as the crowds gather in the fields to witness our latest miracles? Vendors hawk T-shirts in the fields, they sell sodas and popcorn in boxes, and a band starts up, all harp and trumpet, and here comes the evening news, the cameras and the reporters and the makeup artists. But we don't need any makeup, because we're aglow, our skin as pure as water from the darkest, coldest spring. When they turn their cameras on us, they find that we're invisible. Or rather that the light shining through us is so bright it erases everything, even the sky, as if the sun has come to earth and obliterated the landscape. We have our stories, all of us martyrs, our stories of sacrifice and mystical encounters. We speak to each other in tongues unintelligible. We lay healing hands upon each other's blindnesses. We all fall down in flashes of divine incomprehension. We all rise healed of our sinfulness. We, the martyrs, with the powers of martyrs, we are almost floating now, because our holiness is not of this world. But after the vendors and the cameras and the reporters and the makeup artists are gone, when we leave the fields and enter our own houses, our holiness makes us mean. We yell at our children, our spouses, we hide in the garage. Because it's so heavy, the holiness, and we walk bent at the waist from the weight of it, and our necks hurt from holding it up, and we long to throw it off, but we can't.

THAT SUMMER

That summer I got my period and dreamed a man. He was tall, gray-headed and muscular, with kind serious eyes and sensitive hands, hands that could catch an egg without it breaking. Tan skin, good taste in trousers. I named him Adam, naturally, and he kept me company many a night. He laughed at my jokes. He dried my tears. He gave me treasures and never asked to be repaid. He clapped and cheered when I did well, picked me up when I fell. He brought me flowers, sent me love letters. He tied my hands to the bedpost, but only when I wanted him to. He never got angry with me, never lost patience with me, never rolled his eyes at me, never scolded me. In short, he wrecked my life, this Adam I dreamed into being. No man could live up to his promise, though I kept waiting at the door, eagerly, like a well-trained hound. Every time a man walked through, I looked into his eyes and saw Adam, and every time I learned, only too late, that it was not Adam; it was someone else, anyone else. No wonder I was so bereft. This was years ago. Now I'm gray-headed myself. Soon enough I'll have my last period, though I still sometimes dream of Adam, my first man, ruinously fantastic, heroic, as solid as ice is before you have it in your hands.

WHAT SOUNDS

What sounds like rain is tires on asphalt. What sounds like sunlight is death in the trees.

MOVE THAT HATCHET

Move that hatchet, get that fire going, pour the tea, sugar please, make up the bed, cover all the windows and the mirrors, lock up the knives and the silver, because they're coming, armies of them marching in formation with their jackhammer steps and their practical guides to the local flora and fauna and their ancient almanacs turned to the last century, and we in our kitchens with our cats sleeping on the sills, our pies bubbling in our ovens, our boots drying in our mud rooms, this sleepy town, this sleepy day, all sliced to pieces by that sound, the sound of the march, like the sound of a butcher's knife sharping through bone and meat, and the almost cheerful twinkle of their approach, the metallic waves of bayonet tips and medals, the sunlight angling through the ranks in light-colored sleeves, and the wind carrying them in their boots far from home. Are we meant to welcome them? Are we meant to feed them? Because some of theirs look like ours, and some of ours look like theirs. Ever since we heard about the advance, we've been waiting, half in dread, half in childish anticipation, as if it were a circus coming to town, with clowns to entertain us, and I suppose in a way they are, these lads in their costumes and props, just look at how they've rehearsed that march, so in sync, and that expression on their faces, so uniformly numb, so lifelike.

IN *the* WHITE ROOM

WE'RE MARCHING

We're marching out to sea, out to sea and sand and sky, though we don't know where the currents will take us. We're marching out to sea, our feet moving in an eerie unison, as if the whole army of us were one body, and we hardly speak as we soldier forward to the distant smell of salt and spray. We're marching over hills, over flatlands, over wetlands, we're marching over wastelands, in formation through forest upon forest, where the trees part to let us pass, as if they mean to spare our lives, or theirs. On and on we march because the marching, well, it's not for our health that we do it and it's not to please our superiors, though it does please them, so it happens, but the marching, we do it because we want our legs to love the land, we want our legs to claim the soil underfoot, we want to step over all the strangers' graves and find ground that hasn't been overturned. There's no stopping us, is there, and children line the roads, they wave their small handkerchiefs and run after us in their bare feet and short pants and the boys throw flowers and the girls throw rocks, and we gather them up as the trees open into sky and the lane opens into sand. Birds cry overhead, they cry into the night like mothers following the dead, and we cry, too, while we march. The birds ahead circle like predators, they circle and circle like spinning clouds, black and white and gray, like a thickening storm the birds circle, their cries the cries of an ancient locomotive starting up after years, pulling us crawlingly, shriekingly toward the horizon as we march to the sea, which lies just over the ridge, the sand on the hillside pulling at our boots, and when we glimpse that first fringe of rolling blue, we reach into our pockets for the petals and stones.

IN THE WHITE ROOM

In the white room with its white shutters, its white sheets, its white shadows, all the hissing and roaring, all the dreams and the doors—are they locked? Do they open? Where is that draft coming from? Where is everyone?

THE EXILE

When finally he speaks at length, it is about the country he left long ago, in his unhandsome youth, and he addresses that place, that time with a deadened sort of rage, affectionate, vaguely yearnful. The room dims and the waiter lights a candle, which casts a small, imperfect glow across the table at which the exile is consigned to sit, in a crowded upscale restaurant in a village on the wrong side of the ocean. After his recitation the exile is left scowling into his glass, ruing his lost conviction. He is old, with a smile full of troubled yellowing teeth and an unreliable heart and unsound balance, a halting gait. He left his cane at home though, because the exile is proud, and his pride makes him cruel. As does his fear, which is all over him, worse than a shadow, worse than an odor, more like a thought that can't be repressed, a thought stuck in the mind, a thought that begins as a thought but ends as an end, the end, and it's thinking him as he makes jokes at his wife's expense, his friends', the thought thinking the exile, the yellow smile even yellower. When dinner is over he moves away from the table, so slowly, out-of-balance, still joking, but the jokes won't keep him here, nor the tired soliloquies on the literature of the old country, because the thought owns the exile now and a new country is waiting.

LIGHT A CIGARETTE

Light a cigarette for me, old smoker, light it and smoke it down. Pour a drink for me. Make it a double. Drink to my health. Ask me what my name is. Ask me my age. Tell me my fortune. Sing me that song I once liked, the one I thought would change my life. Lead me astray, path of wickedness, lead me away from the narrow and straight, over to the crooked and wide. Show me the wrong way. Teach me the good lies. Find me the best con. Help me cheat and steal my way to a worse place before something nice happens, before I'm praised for my kindness. By the light of this solemn moon I swear to thee that I will forsake thee, grow to hate thee. Thou, with thy winning smile and thy winning ways. I don't intend to keep my promises; I intend to sell them to the highest bidder and walk into the cold, my pockets heavy with gold, and I will think of thee no more, and I will stomp on the graves of all who did me a deed worth doing, because the dirt waits like a widow. So give me that cigarette. And hand me that drink; I'll swallow it at my leisure, though I won't sing for thee. No, not for all the world.

BECAUSE THE SIGN WAS MISSING

Because the sign was missing, we missed the turn and had to turn back, back to a narrow dirt road veering blindly into thickset woods, and as we went, plunging deeper and deeper through the winding tree-shadow, a light rain began to fall. We were searching for the garden, which was somewhere on that road, or so we'd been told. At length we reached a row of gates, but through which gate were we to enter? The Gate of Indecision beckoned, as did the Gate of Felicity, the Gate of Humility, the Gate of Delight, even the Gate of Mirth and Sorrow, since at times we had felt the weight of each. When the rain beat down harder, we ran for the closest gate, the Gate of Chastity. Perhaps we were longing to be pure again. Or perhaps the garden was longing for us, because once we pried open the gate and passed in silence through the stone arch, once we began picking our way over flight after flight of rough hewn steps, the terrain rising and falling under our feet, the trail forking every so often and rambling off through flowering woods, all lush and wild and strange, the rain stopped and we felt a certain heaviness fall away, ourselves lush and wild and strange. We had no idea where we were or where we were going but wandered in a spirit of suspended expectation, letting the stones lead. The garden was in full bloom and smelled of the sweetness of turned earth. Above our heads trees arched like ribs in a cathedral ceiling, and birdcall followed us, as did the whispered conversation of water. Around every corner we came upon a startling new scene, like set pieces in a drama, each with its own intricate tapestry of leaf and blossom, its own body of water, a fishpond or wading pool or fountain or waterfall, and always a place to sit, an encouragement to stop, to rest, to contemplate. Often there was a long banquet table surrounded by chairs, as if at any moment a feast might appear, the table crammed with goblets of wine and steaming platters, the chairs clamoring with rivals and friends, if only we wished it. We wandered over bridges, in and out of tree houses, through multistoried towers, a room hidden behind a waterfall, a giant chess board, its massive wooden kings and queens poised for battle. As the sun climbed down rungs of low-slung clouds, the whispers of water ceased. Someone had turned off the fountains, the waterfalls. In the ensuing silence frogs started to sing. We kept to the path until it ended at an expanse of green, which sloped down to the lake. Slipping off our shoes, we tiptoed barefoot over the cool grass and shucked our clothes and lowered ourselves into the lake, which was as warm as tub water. We swam past the rope swing, past the wooden pier and the barge, past the tiny island crowned with table and chairs, past the floating dock, past the bluffs and the dam, past the canoes and kayaks, swam in that murky warmth all the way out to childhood. Not the childhood of our past but our future childhood, the childhood the garden had given us, the childhood we still dreamed of sometimes, curled up alone in our beds, with their creased sheets and creaking springs.

WHAT SOUNDS

What sounds like music is the insect approach of twilight. What seems like joy is panic. What smells like summer is burning meat. If you wake up and you don't know where you are for a moment, are you lost? If you wake up hating the body beside you, are you stuck?

GIVE THE CHILD A KNIFE

And she'll stab you with it. Give the child an ax and she'll cut off your head. Give the child a cliff and she'll push you over. Give the child a thread and she'll strangle you. Give the child an elevator and she'll send you to the basement. She'll sever the elevator cables, lock the stairs, block the airshafts and turn off the lights. Give the child a pair of shears and she'll cut off your ears. She'll cut off your feet. She'll cut out your belly. Give the child a book and she'll tear out the pages and paper over your face. Give the child a leash and she'll walk you. When you're tired, she'll walk you some more. She'll walk you to the ends of the earth, and she'll leave you there, tied to a fire hydrant at the ends of the earth, with nothing nearby but an empty bowl. Give the child a gun and she'll shoot you in the heart. Give the child a rubber band and she'll make you a slingshot and she'll give it to you as a gift, see? This is the child being nice, as all children are. The rest of it was just a joke. Here's a slingshot. You deserve it for being such a good dad. Take it, it's yours. But the slingshot isn't really a slingshot. It's a grenade that only looks like a slingshot, and the grenade blows up in your hands. Because you weren't a good dad, were you? No, you were bad.

ENJOY THE MAYHEM

Enjoy the mayhem! Mayhem like you've never seen, chaos in the streets, alarms howling, fights and fires breaking out in flash after glorious flash, the neighborhoods emptying out, the bars full of revelers, car windows smashed, the parks reeking of piss, the schools pocked with bullet holes. Enjoy the mayhem, enjoy it while it lasts because the boss is in town, waiting on the hilltop. And thank heaven, he's selling all the good old values, pride in the homeland, loyalty and fealty, flags and pinstripes, family first, bloodthirst. The boss and the men behind him. Luckily they're restoring law and order, and soon, after the dust settles. More police, more riot gear, more lawyers, more prisons, more judges, more arrests. They'll export the criminals, all the bad guys and their bad deeds, the dark-skinned riffraff, the hook-nosed riffraff, returned to sender post haste. The men will climb into their uniforms, the army men, the business men, the church men, their uniforms marching them in file up the avenues, and the ladies will giggle and swoon, and the gentlemen will bow with a creaking sound, and the rich will retrieve their riches from their safes. Before every game the boss will sing our anthem, hand on his heart, to cover up his bald spot. Everyone will cheer, we'll be safe at last, from the riffraff and the mayhem and the past, safe even from the future, and our children will thank us for never having to grow up.

THERE ARE TWENTY-THREE STEPS

There are twenty-three steps to the top of the tower, and I count as I climb. When I reach number twenty-three, I am not, after all, at the top, and there are more to go, twenty-three at least, so I keep climbing. Wind skates through the tower, thin blades of cold edging by my ears with a shirring sort of sound, as if the cold were sharpening, silvering, and the tower seems to recede into the cold. Or maybe those are clouds, moving across the top of the tower and hiding it from view. I didn't know I was this far up; if I look down, it seems just a few steps to the bottom. I continue to climb, twenty-three more into the thinner upmost air, and my feet make the strangest sound as I ascend, like hammers ringing on tin, a dull echoing with a metallic vibration. I try to time each step with the beating of my heart, but the faster I climb the slower my heart beats. Or maybe it's the other way around, I'm not sure, because it's getting harder to breathe the more steps that spiral behind me, like a flag endlessly unfurling. That sound, it reminds me of something from a horror movie, except that no one is behind me, I'm alone on the stairs, climbing another twenty-three. Why am I doing this? I heard the view from the top was very fine. Those who got there swear to it. They say nothing beats the sight of the landscape below, the hills like knuckles on a child's hand and the trees like smudges of ink and the streets like lines traced on paper and the cars crawling along as if they were tiny insects and the houses like shells scattered over a beach. And the people, why, from up here they are so small you can't see them at all.

WHEN YOU DRIVE

That pile of metal, it will own you. When you pierce your ear, the hole will never close. When you leave, you will never come back. If you major in that subject, you will never have any prospects. That job will lead nowhere. That job will be a social torment. That job will last two days. That job won't be a line on your resume. That school you're applying to, the only one, so you can delay or avoid adulthood? That place will be a sterile, unfriendly, soulless hell, where you will learn a great deal of useless information and make a great deal of needless trouble and graduate years later with a fistful of degrees and a dissertation no one will read. Place your hand on that book and solemnly swear. When you take that ring, your life will never be the same. That husband will not want to mother you. That husband will give you a baby. Here, take that small, defenseless creature, the one you just pushed out for ninety-nine hours, he's yours now, and you won't have a moment to yourself for years. That child will inherit your faults, and he will gift them back to you on a daily, no, hourly basis. When you climb onstage with that conjurer, he will cut you in half. Time and again he will escape from the shackles you call an embrace. He will make you disappear. Those people, they will destroy you. Those people, they will save you.

THE ILLUSIONIST

The audience laughs, gasps, applauds. The illusionist learns better tricks, and the audience applauds longer, louder. The illusionist invents ever more elaborate tricks, polishes the patter, seems to risk his life, even, for the applause. It doesn't take much to maintain, just a lot of smoke and a mirror or two, or better yet, bluster and charm, not to mention the repetition of a spell, the words ever more persuasive, then throw in some jokes, a flirtation here and there. With enough drive and hard work the illusionist creates effects so special, so spectacular that everyone starts believing in the magic, and as long as the illusionist sustains the illusion, keeps blowing smoke over the rapt believers, who are always eager for another vanishing, another explosion, then reality is renewed, day after day, year after year. Eventually they forget the illusionist was ever an illusionist; now they call him a mystic. They shout out his name, throw roses and lingerie, brandish their pens for autographs, because his name will live on forever. It's exhausting keeping the magic alive, though, and watch out if the audience ever gets restless.

ONLY NOW

Only now do you notice your face, a mask with no holes, solid as a plate and perfectly shaped to fit over your features, and without holes you can't see or hear or speak, but the mask sees for you, hears and speaks for you, the mask this blighted color we call white, such a devilment, white, the color of unstoppable brightness, brightness of annihilation and erasure, that blinding flash just after the bomb drops, when life crosses over into permanent pause, that liminal upfloating to no one, nowhere. Once the invisible starting line, inaudible starting gun, shade of blissful un-self-awareness; now a tattered flag that waves without a hand to grasp it, no finger to pull the trigger, no fist to tighten the noose. A heaviness, and why not? Darkness not the only urn poured full of bad dreams, daylight a bad dream of its own, and we itch with that bad dream, we itch across our body, we toss at all hours in the bed we made, white sheets, white comforter, white heaviness, our arms tremble from trying to hold it up, we ramble bent over, straining to see the footprints vanishing behind us, we stagger inside our pale overlying, inside the mask, the armor, the winter coat, skin we can't stop scratching, skin pared away from the flesh, our paper house with its peeling walls, our heaviness holding us up, holding us down, our ruin.

NIGHTFALL

WHEN IT HITS YOU

When it hits you that your face is missing, peeled back from your skull-front like a lavish window display lifted from a fancy shop, you can do nothing; it's already long gone. And you weren't even aware of the loss, because your face disappeared while you were distracted, admiring the scenery. Like that summer in Avignon, on a stroll along the Rue de la Balance, and before you knew it, a throng of roaming women had you surrounded; they clawed at your purse and taunted you. That time you managed to hold on to your possessions. This time, no such luck, your face gone in an instant, and you had no idea until you saw it staring back at you with those eyes, your eyes, burning blue, and that plaintive ravaged expression, your expression, the one that comes over you when it hits you anew, that your face has been taken, that your sadness has been taken, your longing and regret, your shame, your youth, your sense of your own beauty, your pride—all taken, all peeled away. Who could have done this to you? Was it someone you knew or a stranger? Your best friend in the world? An enemy, perhaps, though at this point could you tell the difference? Or were you the culprit? By not paying attention, by trusting in good intentions, assuming the best, but whatever the case, whoever the taker, your face is gone, and it's never coming back. You walk around faceless, clutching your jawbones, your cheekbones with a tender vigilance, because you need bones to face whatever's coming, you need something hard to absorb the impact of the next blow.

SOMEDAY I MUST TELL

It's not a pretty story, just as I'm no longer pretty, and it needs to be told to survive. But I'm not going to tell it to you now, as we walk along the boulevard, arm in arm, the sun hovering at the horizon like a stalled conversation, people in their evening finery strolling past, the men in top hats and tails, the women in glittering gowns, tiaras riding crests of hair at their temples, their fingers flashing with jewels, their wrists and collarbones flashing, and their easy smiles as they nod with that mutual recognition. Because look at us, we're in love and decked out in our finest, you in your tux, which strains around the belly despite your efforts at moderation, and me in my crinkled silver dress, like the foil around a baked potato but timelessly stylish somehow. And the ring on my finger, that huge improbable diamond my mother gave to you to give to me. When after nine months you didn't, she took it back, had it reappraised and gave it to me herself. Does that mean I'm technically promised to my mother? Maybe, but what's so strange about that? We were always promised, my mother and I, an unholy couple, like most mothers and daughters. Maybe you knew. Maybe that's why you put the ring in the top drawer of your dresser, along with your passport and the medal your father won. Maybe you knew if you gave me the ring, you would have to be my mother.

THE JAILS

The jails, they're full of prisoners. Why are they full of prisoners? Because everyone's doing drugs or selling them. Why is everyone doing drugs or selling them? Because they're bored and desperate. Why are they bored and desperate? Because they have no work. Why don't they have work? Because the jobs went away. Why did the jobs go away? Because the bosses put in robots. Why did the bosses put in robots? Because robots don't ask questions.

Why don't robots ask questions? Because they don't have minds. Why don't they have minds? Because the scientists haven't gotten that far. Why haven't the scientists gotten that far? Because the government won't fund them. Why won't the government fund them? Because they're funding the army. Why are they funding the army? So we can fight. Why should we fight? Because we have enemies. Why do we have enemies? Because we're always interfering. Why are we interfering? Because we're better than they are. Why are we better than they are? Because we're free. Why are we free? Because we waged a war to worship our own gods. Why did we wage a war to worship our own gods? Because we felt oppressed. Why did we feel oppressed? Because they put us in the jails.

IN THE WHITE ROOM

Why am I lying here, bent nearly in half? What am I afraid of? It's an ordinary day, as far as I know, but the sun looks inflamed behind the shutters. And the world seems to be moving briskly, though everything here is still. In the white room light bleeds in from outside, where the streets have forbidding names and unforgiving faces and unfamiliar signs. I wish I could stand up. I wish I could straighten myself out. I wish I could walk through these walls or summon someone, but I'm here alone, and the air is muffled and the sound is cold and the light is clotted and the walls are so white, the ceiling white, two white pillows stacked on an empty trunk, the shutters spattered in white.

BLAME NO ONE

Blame no one but yourself for all this. Blame no one else, because no matter how badly your luck fell out, how dastardly fate planned against you, and how twisted the conspiracies that kept you from your various vanquishments—of the handsomest suitors, the plummest missions, the world itself, the flat unmappable world—it was always you at fault. What did you do wrong? Did you start at the wrong starting line? Eat the wrong breakfast? Take the wrong vitamins? Dream the wrong dreams? Say the wrong hellos, the wrong farewells? Stay in the wrong relationships, the wrong situations? Leave the right ones? Sit on the wrong benches in the wrong parks in the wrong cities in the wrong seasons in the wrong century? Could you have changed a thing? Did you ignore the signs? The signs were there, right in front of you, practically strapped onto your wrist, like a watch handed down to you by the great-grandmother you never knew, the second hand ticking round and round with a tsking sound, the very sound your mother made when you wore something she didn't like, or said something she didn't like, or even thought something she didn't like. Maybe that was the problem all along, that you thought the wrong thoughts, the thoughts that got you in trouble whether you liked it or not. And often you did. Like it, that is, because trouble was so much more interesting, more damaging. That's right, blame only yourself, no one was forcing you to think those thoughts, the ones that kept you up nights, the ones that made you snarl and weep and tear at your hair, the ones that put a smile on your lips, like a cat that claws the goldfish out of the bowl and swallows it whole.

MUST SHE ALWAYS

Must she always have to beg? Of course, she must. He prefers her small, so she begs. But she's grown tired of it, grown tired of the pleading, tired of diminishing, and she longs to stop. It was always just an act anyway. She doesn't need to beg to get what she wants; she simply goes after it in her underhanded way. Yes, she's aware that at a certain point it has nothing to do with her, the script she's performing, but it's so strange to be performing it still, after all these years, as if every time were the first time, as if she's feeling it or believing it, and he believing, too, but it's only words, or at least she hopes it is, and she keeps wondering when it will be over, how many words later, so she can walk back into her proper body and abandon the body that's expected to beg, the body that speaks and speaks, the body betraying itself, that made-up body with the mouth pulled by a string. By now she almost has to laugh, she's begged so many times. And for what? So he can imagine beating her, besting her for once, isn't that right? Because it's all a dream from first word to last, that chance to become her, and she become him, though it's sad when it's over, to have to return to himself again.

IF ONLY I COULD TAKE

If only I could take my head off for a while. If only I could put it on the nightstand or in a jar. I could give my neck a break, give my brain a break from all the troublesome thinking. With my head on the nightstand or in a jar, my heart would be in charge, my hands and feet the heart's deputies, and I would feel my way everywhere, without any thought. Lacking a head I would probably put something else on my neck, so as not to alarm the neighbors. A tropical shrub might do. My features would blossom seasonally, my vine-hair grow long in the sun. Even better: one of those plants with sticky-spiked mouths that snap up insects. That way I could stay a carnivore, even without my head. Or maybe something more fanciful, a paper lantern with a tea candle inside. At night I could light the candle, and my lantern head would lift off my body and into the darkness like a jellyfish rising through water. But what would I do for eyes with my head in the clouds? Do I need eyes? To see what? A little blindness might do this body good, because it never hurts to develop one's inward sight, or so say the sages. I can already feel the release, the headless freedom of nothing on my mind, no brain, no senses, no sense. I can hardly wait. Maybe I'll just leave my neck unadorned, like an uncapped pipe, and people can drop coins down the pipe for good luck, close their eyes and make their wishes.

ON THE BRINK OF THIS

On the brink of this silvering place you sit and stare at the ground losing shape at your feet. The mountains loom behind you, like ancestors glaring down from the past at the messes you've made. The night, though not yet permanent, threatens to last past all reason. Not the darkness but the restless emptiness, the quiet, the all-but-aloneness. As you sit and stare, you sink into it, the immensity that rises with the moon, the feeling that the world is uncaring, unseeing, that the world wants to keep you in the cheap seats with a warm beer and a cold hot dog, that all you have going for you is a beating heart and two shaky legs to take you nowhere, or at least to the brink of nowhere, where you'll sit and stare, still clutching that beer, and watch night take the field. Not the darkness but the sense that creatures are coming out, creatures that emerge only in shadow. They creep among the weeds, they creep tentacled and groping, uncaring, unseeing, and make for all your open parts, your moist parts, the softest swathes of skin, the veins, the bruises, and they bite before you know they're there. They bite you and vanish, like all the petty cruelties heaped upon you by those who love you best.

NIGHTFALL

When I look up at the mountains, where the fog has gathered like a wedding veil and the sky has settled close. When I gaze across the flowering meadow where the fireflies flit from stalk to stalk. When I close my eyes and open them again, the evening waiting just offstage, the knees beneath me trembling, the silence majestic and stark. When the mountains fade behind the fog like a passion grown stale, and the clouds gather like guests at the sacrament, and the sun behind the horizon a priest waiting to perform the rite. When the last day-bird sings and the last squirrel ascends the last branch. When the cars plow through the darkness and rumble over the bridge. When the river hardens into the stone of darkness and night-birds peep out of the shadows. When the biting flies dart from leg to leg and the biting spiders creep out of the cracks. When the corners lose their angles and the marshes glow like tar. When I gather up my limbs, hanging from their sockets like flags without a wind. When I fold them with the tenderness of a penitent. When I put them in the cupboard and close the cupboard door, only then does the fog clear, as if the rings have been exchanged, the vows spoken, the priest declaring the couple joined in holy union, and the groom lifts the veil to kiss the bride, only there is no bride, just the sky's face, her eyes clouded over.

OUT IN THE COUNTRY

Out in the country the tree comes alight every night with fireflies, and the sky glows a cool blue, like a painting of loneliness, and the birds fly in from days gone by. They land in the branches of the evening, singing of their darkening business, and the air grows heavy with song, like a blanket soaked with rain. We're sitting out on the deck, two aging solitaries, and our wars wage on noiselessly between us even as we breathe in the twilight air. How did we get here from the paradise where we met? How did we move from that original garden, that original tree with its thick, dark trunk to this tree, stark and slightly aloof, its leaves trembling in the falling dusk, the fireflies blinking in its crown like constellations? How can we sit so close without touching? How can the night not act upon us like a miracle? But we're immune; we've seen this play before, this night, this slow, setting sun. And you wonder at the stillness of the clouds as if for the first time. And I wonder at your wonder, the same wonder as yesterday and the day before. As I sit beside you, I keep receding, and you stare ahead, since ahead is the only place you can see. My watch is slow, like the dusk, and fireflies flit among the leaves like stars blinkered by the darkness, the light and shadow changing every moment, the way we are, though it feels like we'll be this way forever.

WE RETURN TO THE CITY

We return to the city lugging our suitcases and our heartache, the escalator cranking us up from underground, the station mobbed, throbbing in the artificial light of urbanity. We thread ourselves through the headless throngs with teeth gritted, and though it's summer outside we shrug our toughness back on like a winter coat. We drift downstairs to the subway as though we were sleepwalking, too stunned to open our eyes. And why should we? The city is shrill and seething, incessant, the sky the color of concrete, the concrete the color of mud, and the subway heaves away from the station, wheezing us from this purgatory to the next. We hold hands with what's left of our pastoral sympathy as the train burrows under the city, under the river. The other passengers look folded, faded, crumbling, like paper bags left out in the rain, the skin on our fingers and our palms creased and crumpled under the train's unblinking fluorescence. When we emerge into daylight again, the streets greet us with indifference, as if they've seen our kind before and know we'll come around eventually, back to the rush, the shove, the slight waiting at throat's edge. We round the corner feeling numb, as if some terrible news has been broken to us, and it has. We're home.

SENT IN THE MAIL

Sent in the mail it was, my heart in a paper cage, sent over the ocean in a steamer. It made a long journey, by the light of a wide ocean sun, a waning moon and the stars, remote and inscrutable, the stars in their star shapes, and when it landed at the port it was bundled onto a horse and buggy and trundled over cobblestones, over city lanes and out to desert, to a dry starless night, to the wolfbark and snakebite, and it crossed the desert in a freight train, and the sand blew along the tracks and the train whistled across the sand like a boy alone in the dark, the train pushing into the station with a heavy sigh, and it was loaded onto a wagon drawn by two mares, sisters past their prime, and the wagon bumped over roots and ruts, along the knotted road under a thick canopy of leaving branches, and the shadows were green and the sun was the white of an eye, and the mares pulled into the post office, where it was piled on a bicycle, and the bicycle spun along a dry river bed across a meadow blooming with vines, and birdsong pecked holes in the sky and the shadows were a cool blue and the sun was the orange of the beach and drops of water clung to the vines and trembled with orange light, and it crossed the chirruping meadow, reaching the house just as the sun was cresting the roof, and it slipped into the slot in the entry hall and settled on the marble tile, just adjacent to the parlor, where it jolted awake, roaring and rearing, talons flared, rattling the bars.

ENJOY the MAYHEM

I WENT SEARCHING

I went searching for my heart in the hollow of birds, the hollow where my lost loves had alighted, searching for the music where the leaves of their singing bloomed, and soon the air grew nearly solid with their notes, so that I was forced to stand still, to brace myself against it as against a strong wind, the air thick with the strands of it, like braided hair, and my hands combed blindly through the air, notes threading through my fingers, the melodies so familiar and faraway I could have stood there all night listening, in the darkness, which was alive with that song, and aquiver, as if charged with electricity, as if sparks were igniting around me, all through my fingers, and loneliness bent my head and pushed me further into the hollow, through the singing air, and the song closed around me, like curtains upon curtains, as if the hollow were a world of windows with no walls, no floors or ceilings, just panes through which all darkness become visible, a darkness woven thick, which shook with song and muffled my breath, and I found myself facing windows opening onto more windows, the darkness reeling and roiling, the song like a skullcap, like a shawl around my shoulders, a rug under my feet, alone in the bird hollow. But where were the birds? The birds had flown.

WHAT SOUNDS

What sounds like silence is anger. Look, over there, it's your father and grandfather and their fathers and grandfathers and so on, lining up, arms akimbo, across a field in a game of Red Rover, and they're calling your name, calling you to come over. Is it a taunt? An invitation? Whatever it is, you're off and running, like always, across the wild grasses, your breath puffing like smoke from a locomotive, the wind ripping through your hair. What's happening to your hair? It's turning brown again, your legs nimble and firm, pounding over the grasses, and your neck holding up your head like a sunflower's stem, all your movements easy and painless, as if you've been released from gravity, and as you run, your fathers and grandfathers join hands. They tense their legs and set their faces, because they're not letting you break through. This time they want to win.

I LIFT MY HANDS

I lift my hands to the air, checking for vibrations. I listen under my pillow. I open all my ears. I'm waiting for my ancestors to speak to me, but they're so dead, and I hear nothing, not a peep. Why have they abandoned me? Have I offended them? Am I not living right? They must feel no connection to me, no need to wake up from the dream of time and send me counsel. It's true, I speak a different language than they did, and I live in a different land; I don't believe in their religion and never learned their rituals. Perhaps they hold all this against me and are punishing me with their silence, like the God of ancient grudges. Pity, I could use a few pointers, here in the world of ongoing modernity, especially as it keeps flying past, like a cross-country train for which I have no ticket. I'll wager there was at least one sage among my mighty dead, a healer or a prophet or a ruler, though at this point I'd settle for a swindler, any old-timer willing to spare a word about making more effective decisions, or timing my timing in a more timely way, a plan for getting ahead, cutting in line, wrangling a ticket for that train, the train of the twenty-first century, which is speeding toward the edge of the world as fast as its wheels can spin. But my ancestors are silent in their graves, as silent as the dirt you turn over in your child-sized fists, in search of heirlooms buried in the backyard.

GOD, I CAN'T STAND

God, I can't stand all these tiny outstretched hands. What are they asking for? I haven't a nickel, no change whatsoever, and if they think I'll give them anything today, they've got another thing coming. I just want to be left alone. I just want to wake up and walk out into the day-old world without feeling those hands on me, their empty open palms so pale, as pale as glass and hot to the touch. How alive they are, their hearts beating up through their wrists, and their lacks bigger than their souls. Why do they think I have anything for them? And what, finally, do they want? I've emptied my wallet time and again, and still they keep coming, those hands, with the soft cushy pads below their thumbs. I have so little, and what I have I'd rather keep. Is it my fault they need so much? What if I had nothing? They'd ask for that, too. They'd ask for my nothing, they'd find a way, and I'd probably give it to them, because a woman sees all the tiny outstretched hands even when her eyes are closed. She sees them and she can't ignore them, she can't forget them, and she gives them what she has every time, not because she has so much, but because they ask. And she is answering before the question is finished, answering despite herself, to spite herself, because as soon as she answers, they ask again. The hands open, empty every time, their softness like a prayer to a god they know will answer.

BOMBS AWAY

Bombs away, old boys, what are you waiting for? Bombs away! Don't worry about what's ahead of you, or above you, or even below you. Don't worry about what's in your wake, just keep your head on straight and let 'er rip, lads, because the war's on and anything goes, as they say. Take no prisoners and up, up, and away, through the yonder and into the enemy, though everyone's the enemy these days. At least, they could be, you never know. You meet them on the street, dressed funny or dressed like you. Heck, they could be your cousins but also your mortal foes, so you better get ready. Get your hands on your holsters and your hearts in high gear, 'cause there's gonna be a fight, folks, whether you like it or not. There's always a fight happening somewhere, might as well be here. You won't believe our technology, once we get it running. We go from zero to sixty before we know we're moving, that's how fast, how powerful we are. So watch out, don't piss us off, mack, because we're mighty and we're fierce and we're oh-so-piss-off-able, and we need nothing more than a cough in the wrong direction to set us off. With our engines running and our wings flapping and our tickers ticking we have to go forward, go toward, go up and away. We're burning through all our fuel and all yours, so cover your mouth and keep your heads down, lads. 'Cause you never know when it'll be you up there, your finger on the trigger, never know when it'll be too late to come down, too late to stop, too late to bring it back.

I FOUND MYSELF

I found myself in a temple at the top of a mountain on one of the islands, where I wandered, spellbound. Time hadn't touched the temple's ornate frescoes and grand columns, its beauty overwhelming in the way of relics massive and ancient. The walls trembled with the power of this beauty, and a strange light seemed to emanate from the altar, a holy light, and smoke wafted from the rafters as if the heavens were burning. As my feet padded soundlessly over the tiles, a music came over me, a choir so heartbreakingly soaring and wild that I grew frightened. I sensed something was growing in me, as if a seed had taken root in the desert, and I moved as if chosen, soundlessly, up to the altar. As soon as I mounted the steps, I felt my legs drop out from under me and my arms spread to catch my fall, but I was floating, removed from my senses, dazed, filling with a fire as sharp and hot as a newly forged sword, a burning that seared me from inside, I could smell myself burning, blood seeping from my pores, flesh in tatters, eyes blistered, though my heart kept beating as that beauty ebbed the life out of me.

MEANWHILE AN ANGEL

Meanwhile an angel appeared. A man angel, all clean-shaven and smelling of cigarettes, and he was wearing white robes, like angels in movies. He seemed none too pleased about it, having to wear white robes. He seemed more like a jeans-and-T-shirt kind of angel, an angel who shaved only for job interviews and seeing his in-laws. But there he was, on the corner of Stanton and Ludlow in his white robes and gleaming chin, and he said, "I have the power to make your wishes come true." He said this to me. Then he added, "But I'm not going to." And I said, "Seriously?" And he said, "Ha, I'm not joking. I could make you famous and wealthy and an object of the utmost admiration, blah, blah, blah. But I'm not going to." And I said, "Why not?" And he said, "I just don't feel like it." And I said, "Then why are you here? Why are you telling me this?" And he said, "This is my corner. I've been here for decades. And I'm telling you this so you'll know." And I said, "Well, that's pretty rotten. I'd rather not know that my wishes were in my grasp but denied by a clean-shaven hipster in a toga." And he said, "What? You don't like my look? I thought it was ironic." "I like it," I admitted. "But I don't like you. You remind me of my ex-boyfriend, somehow." "Not my fault," he said. "I remind everyone of their ex-boyfriend. It's one of my qualities." "How did you die?" I asked him. "I killed myself," he said. "Why?" I asked. "Because an angel in white robes made all my wishes come true," he replied. "What a nightmare. This was in San Francisco, back in the seventies."

BUT HER FEATURES

But her features were falling off her face and her lap was sliding off her legs and her voice shifted, as if the ground were dropping away, and she slipped inside her skin a little, as if the mask were too big, and the air rippled with voices and the clatter of clean plates and the clink of glasses, To your health! No, to yours! and the laughter sounded televised and the music blared with an oppressive pulse, as if a surgeon had opened up the room with a pair of shears and its heart were thumping out the beat, while ballad after ballad beamed back from the wayward '90s, and her glasses slid to the floor and the bartender stepped on them without a word, and the air grew dark, as if she had entered a tunnel, but it was only night surrounding her, as if she had been hunted down, as if night had been waiting there all day, just around the corner, and that smile she flashed at the bartender over the lemons and the limes, why did it look like a fist, still clinging to her chin?

VERY GOOD

Very good, said the butter. Very good, said the jam. Very good, said the toast. Very good, said the toaster. Not so good, said the waitress. My husband left me, took up with his ex-wife. She's younger than I am and prettier, too. Very good, said the jam. Very good, said the butter. Not so good, said the cook. I'm in debt. To my bookie, my son-in-law and my dentist. And God, too, I owe him a pack of cigarettes and nineteen hundred bucks. Don't ask; it was just this thing that went wrong between us. Very good, said the toaster. Very good, said the toast. Very good, said the fat man who ate the toast. This toast is very good. The butter, it's very good. The jam, also very good. Very good, said the butter inside the fat man's stomach. Very good, said the jam. Very bad, said the toast. I miss the toaster.

NECESSARY ILLS

Necessary ills, necessary suffering, all around us, flooding the streets. And they're dropping like flies, all the people over there, countries of strangers fighting in the squares, a new revolution every day, new blood, new stock photographs, all of it necessary for the evolution of history and society and the world economy. And we're waiting for the one thing, waiting for someone to press a button, for something beloved to explode in the most spectacular way, captured on film and played again and again on every channel, because that's entertainment, the explosions and the blood, though we're a bit sorrier if it's real, truly we are. But it must happen, the necessary ills spilling through the avenues like flooding sewers, the stink of them, the rising tides. If only I had a button to press, then I might possess some small crumb of power, which I could trade for prestige, which I could trade for a good opinion or two, which I could trade for a few minutes of fame, which I could trade for a little more power, a fancy detonator with a red button, something in gold I could wear around my neck. Everyone would fear me, fear the necessary ills inside my box, ills I could let fly as soon as I pressed the button. I could walk the world this way, with power at my fingertips, and people would greet me with fearful eyes and wide smiles. They would run to greet me and fling themselves at my feet, and I wouldn't feel loved, no, but I would feel real.

IN THE WHITE ROOM

My hands clutch this notebook as if it were the hand of my father, dying of a self-inflicted gunshot wound to the head. He was in a white room of his own. Or was it night in there? Hard to tell, his eyes were so opaque.

THE APOCALYPSE HAS HAPPENED

The apocalypse has happened, everyone agrees, and I'm reading about it in the paper. APOCALYPSE HAS HAPPENED, the headlines say; IT'S THE END OF THE WORLD, says the news, but it's strange, everything looks the same, the sun is still beaming and the shadows are still leaning and people are rushing off to work and the mail is being delivered. But everyone's talking about the end of the world. Why now? Why today? It's rather inconvenient, isn't it, with all the plans we made. Why look, even I have a full calendar today. I'm getting my teeth cleaned in the morning, and lunch with Greg at 1:00, and Louis will expect me in the office after that, then dinner with Jeff at 7:30 and perhaps we'll catch a movie, if that sequel is still playing. I was going to get a new car. I was going to have some yard work done. I was going to get a new pair of boots. I was going to get a new personality and change my life and become a real success, but time has run out, apparently, and it hasn't improved traffic any. You'd think people would be home with their kids or their aging parents, but no, they're all turning onto Ponce de Leon and lining up at the Majestic. Well, that's something I wouldn't have expected, people still have their appetites. I wish I had mine. Where should I go? My son is away at college, my boyfriend off traveling again. I guess I'll stay here; where else is there? From the nightstand I take a deck of cards, shuffle, deal. I'm playing solitaire at the end of the world. The moon is full, my tiny room immense.

GO BY, GO BY

NO ONE UNDERSTOOD

No one understood how it would be after the apocalypse. Everyone thought there would be war and drought and scrabbling for food and that the cockroaches and spiders would be taking over. But no, quite the contrary. Sure, most everything was destroyed, but what was left was intact. All the grocery stores were full of canned goods and cereals, the malls stocked to the gills with jewels, designer watches, attractive clothing in every size, and the dealerships loaded with luxury cars, all ours for the taking. The few people left were also intact, and more or less sane. When the lot of us met, tensely it seemed, to make some rules and divvy up the stuff, there was more than enough to go around, and the tension eased. We survived with no trouble in that world after the world ended, a world floating in an ocean of comforting possessions, and we were comfortable. The internet was gone, the TVs and radios, even the presses, silent. No president, no government, no infighting. Least of all amongst ourselves. But what were we to do all day except wait for something to happen, wait for one of us to break. Would someone fall in love? Would someone go mad? Alas, no one fell in love and no one went mad. We sat around and ate cereal in our well-fitting mall clothes, and we admired our jewels and our watches, which kept different times, but so what? Our luxury cars ran out of gas, but so what?

THE GREEN

I keep moving but my legs are still. I keep breathing but my lungs are stiff sponges. I keep singing but my jaws are rusted shut. Where have the old prayers gone, the old songs, the colorful flags waving in the breezes? Where are the breezes? I keep waving, but my hands are stuck in my pockets. I keep eating but the food ran out. How did we ever carry on? How did life continue, with its possibilities and its promises? The birds unwinged, the snakes unbellied, the squirrels de-tailed. I keep moving but my feet stay behind. I keep speaking but the words stick in my chest. The ground has gotten so dry, brittle, littered with dust. Remember when the ground was moist, when the green of spring ignited into orange, into gold, and all the withering winter browns? Now the green has settled over us with the dust, settled into an eternal season, like a sickness we can't get rid of, all this never-changing green. I keep standing but my knees won't unbend. I keep sitting but the chairs have crumbled. The ground is parched, I dare not touch it. I keep trying but I have no will. I keep praying but my heart won't budge. And the ground is like ashes under my feet. I keep moving and the green moves with me. The green, the beautiful, terrifying green.

HERE WE ARE

Do you trust me? Do I trust you? No, trust died last century, along with truth, so we'll have to think of something else to shake on. Not to our health. Our health is bad and only getting worse. Not to our wealth. Not to you and yours. Not to me and mine, because yours and mine, every last one, perished in the wars, and without yours there is no you, and without mine there is no me. Just two bodies standing face to face, two envelopes of flesh with nothing folded inside. How did we survive? And better yet how did we emerge heroic after all that carnage, all that betrayal and heartbreak? Loss for every meal, loss before bedtime and on rising. That's why we're empty, because emptiness made us, made these bodies in which we stand, high on the hilltop, under a pallid moon, with the fields of bones surrounding us like a fresh snowfall, except that the heat here is insufferable. Last winter was years ago, before the battles broke out, remember? Here, let's shake on that. To winter. To cold. To snow, real snow.

THE MARKS ON THIS PAGE

The marks on this page signify nothing. They're in a language I don't recognize. How is that possible? It's my language. I speak it, I read and write it, but I've lost my understanding. People open their mouths, sounds come out, and they mean nothing. I look at my family, my friends, my strangers without comprehension, as if they were a school of fish trying to swim outside the current, their mouths flapping, gasping for air. This feeling, it's frightening, certainly, but also freeing. Not to understand anything. As if I've arrived in the foreign country of my life, where not only the language but also the customs seem alien, out of sync. See, there I am, holding my suitcases. I'm standing at the sign on my street corner, but I can't read the sign. I've lost my key, and I know without trying it that the door to my house is locked, and if I snake my hand into the mouth of the watering can, I won't find the spare. Because it's no longer my house, it was only my house when I could understand the language, when I could speak my way inside. I'm afraid to open my mouth, to greet my neighbors, to say my own name. If I can't understand anything, how could anyone understand me? I'm stuck at the corner, at the sign that used to say STOP, holding my suitcases. I'm afraid to put them down, afraid someone will take them, because no one looks friendly here, though they all look familiar, like neighbors I've seen in a film. Not a recent film either, something dated and corny, but popular in its day. Now I wonder if, somehow or other, I've awoken inside this film. If only I had a part to play, someone to save or to betray, but I have nothing to say. If only I could put down these suitcases, I might approach someone, or wave.

GO BY, GO BY

Go by, go by. Reds go by, yellows go by, float away and go by, go by. Blues go by and the greens, too, float away and go by. The dust and the petticoats, the foundlings and the amputees, go by, float away and go by. The world is floating away. Go by, world, go by, off into the outer realms, off into the superfluous futures, which are branching continuous, like ivy sending tendrils across the floorboards. Go by, futures, float away and go by. Raise your sails and skim the waters, jigger and jugger across the ice-cracked oceans, shiver toward the poles, turn blue and liquefy, futures, and go by, go by. Go by, oranges, go by, lemons, drip-drop and go by, past the lemonade stand and the fallen pennies, past the dump with its smell of rot and uselessness, past the old house where the palm tree grew, past the mailbox sinking into earth, past the lake and the stuffed game posed on hind legs, teeth bared, past the gated mansions that used to be a golf course, past the mall and the movie houses and the expressway with its dangerously short on-ramps, go by, go by, float away and go by. We've heard there's a river in town, though we've never seen it, so we stand on the edge of the rumored river and look into the rumored water, into the muck and the rubber, into the weedy wet. Beneath our faces bits of refuse swim by like tiny fluttering fishes, and the greens, there they go, the greens go by, and the browns go by, go by, the darks and the lights go by, float away and go by, our faces wavering over the surface of the current, ourselves spread across the river's roof like so many shingles.

MIRACLE OF MINE

Miracle of mine, how I lie here in my naked finery, half dreaming in the former night of my youth. The clock blinks on and off. Leaf blowers drone in monklike harmony. A dog barks. The sun cheeringly blares through my high windows as if trumpets were announcing the royal procession of my waking. But I haven't woken. At least, not in the metaphorical sense. I'm still asleep, wrinkled across the sheets, legs crossed, skin drooping, hair all agray. Blind, stupid, flabby and useless. And let's not forget the pain, the pain like luggage I'm stuck carrying all day along those endless moving sidewalks that shunt you from one vague place to another. My mouth is glued shut and my ears are gummed up and I'm wiping the dreams from the corners of my eyes. I can hardly see in the merciless light. Now the dread settles over me like a soft rain, with that damp, fresh smell, the dread drying in a film on my skin. Barely perceptible, but it's there all right. Is that what's making my skin so loose? Is that what's turning my hair white? No, that's age, that's time, that's death, creeping up on me like my least favorite playmate, the one I don't remember inviting over. Maybe my mom invited death without asking me first. That would be typical.

THE SHIP HAS SUNDERED

The ship has run aground and there go the rats, every last one scurrying down the gangplank, their rusty tails rattling behind them. There go the rats, they're scattering through the town, which is empty, since the people long ago retreated inland and disappeared inside the jungle. Now the ship is empty, too. Empty, empty, empty. Now the water's seeping in, ebbing and flowing into the cracks and the breaches. The wood's expanding, a slow, leisurely opening out, like a yawn late in the afternoon. Oh, look at the ship, lonely there on the bleak sand-crusted shore, its prow curved like a vulture's beak, the wood rotting, and what doesn't rot will petrify. The ship so empty, the emptiness a kind of beauty, the beauty of the sand and the waves and the rising moon. Because suddenly it is night at the archipelago. Night spills over the edges of the sky like a vat of ink, spills over the sand, spills over the silken waves, spills over the moon. The ship is sighing in its ribs, expanding, taking on water, and the night is truly dark, now that the rats have disappeared into the emptiness. The town closes its eyes. The ship nods. Yes, it says, you can take me over now. I am ready.

THE ISLAND

I swam without ceasing around the rocks guarding the island, the looming black rocks slick with surf. In sunlight they shone like onyx, as if polished. In a storm they were flat and dull as slate. I used to search for an opening in the rocks, some small gap through which to slip my body, in the hopes of finding calmer waters, because the seas were so choppy then, the waves churning as if in anger, the foam roiling up to the rock tips, but the rocks made a wall around the island, a wall that seemed impenetrable. I swam around the rocks with my thrashing crawl—I was never a good swimmer—always wondering where my strokes would take me, the sun overhead like a deity watching my slow progress, scratching its head and muttering, *Why her, why here, swimming in circles?* I could never find a space in the rocks through which the island was visible. I could only imagine a place, wild with raw beauty, running with springs and vines, where the flowers grew as high as trees, the trees high as skyscrapers, where horses galloped on the sand, horses majestic as clouds, leaving sand upturned behind them like trails of sugar, which the waves would wash over, wash away, where blue butterflies and tropical birds dotted the flowers and trees like confetti, and all the fruit I could bear to eat. What a vision, this island. I swam around it for years. If only I'd thought to swim away.

THE SKULL ON MY DESK

The skull on my desk spoke to me this morning. It said, *Why so glum, chum?* and I said, *I don't have a father*, and the skull said, *Why do you need a father?* and I said, *Everyone needs a father*, to which the skull inquired, *What is a father, exactly?* and I said, *A father is someone who is solid and reassuring and warm, with infinite perspective and a gentle sense of humor, and who listens to your problems and responds to them with precisely these qualities*, and the skull said, *It sounds hard to be a father*, and I said, *I should think so*, and the skull said, *Why don't you have a father?* and I said, *Because my father shot himself in the head*, and the skull said, *Gosh, how terrible, I'm sorry*, and I said, *Thanks, it was a long time ago*, and the skull said, *But look how old you are now, your hair is practically half gray and you're getting to be such a wizened little thing*, and I said, *Thanks for pointing that out, I look in the mirror every day*, and the skull said, *Well, I'm just saying, you're all grown up now*, and I said, *Only on the outside*, and the skull said, *Well, then grow up on the inside*, to which I replied, *I'm trying*, and the skull said, *How hard can you be trying?* and I said, *As hard as I can*, and the skull said, *Try harder*, and I said, *That's easy for you to say, you're a skull*, and the skull said, *You don't know anything about me*, and I said, *You're not even real, you were made in a factory, probably in China*, and the skull said, *Who are you to say what's real?* and I said, *Sorry, you're right, I don't know what's real*, and the skull said, *I forgive you*.

THERE I WAS

There I was at the garden party, the sun atremble at trees' edge, the women in fine flowered frocks, the men in straw hats and seersucker, champagne flutes fitted to their lips, rose and azalea bushes dressed buddingly in their best, and behind me the buzz of bees, a good-natured hum hovering over the garden. I set my flute on a glass-topped table and wandered away from the women gathered to gossip and admire, the men talking golf and politics, my skirts feathering across my skin like curtains in the warm, honey-scented breezes, blown in as if to complement the season. I was drowsy, distracted. Unformed notions flashed into consciousness and out again, like the sunlight dappled among the blossoms. Not far from the party I knelt in the cool grass, the bees behind me grown louder, more insistent, the way the murmurings of a restless audience swell in anticipation of a performance. I glanced over my shoulder, and as if they had been waiting, the bees lifted, like dust shook from a tapestry, lifted in a dense veil of noise. Then they came. Like a well-aimed arrow the bees came, buzzing now quite loudly, one might even say angrily. They came for me. I looked back at the party in alarm, tried to stand, to signal the women for help, but no one noticed me, or the bees, which all at once were upon me, and I among them, surrounded so utterly I could no longer see, as if night's lid had closed over the garden. I braced myself to be stung. I dared not move, nor so much as breathe, the bees' heavy drone enwrapping me as a shroud. I thought to pray, but to whom? All of a sudden it was light. I was untouched. Only then did my heart start stuttering in fear, for though the bees had passed me by, the buzzing remained, insistent and pressingly close, as if inside my ears. Before I could exhale, the bees returned, coalescing before me in a cloud the very shape of my kneeling body, like an image in a warped mirror. I stared at this dark reflection with a senseless calm, awestruck and curious, aware of the danger yet helpless in the presence of such a powerful, terrifying beauty—numberless, electric, menacing. Suddenly they scattered, but after a moment they knelt again before me in another droning cloud, this one even thicker, closer. The livid sound of their buzzing was so loud I could hear nothing else, not even my own fear. As we faced one another, I and the bees, I had no thoughts at all, not even of death, which felt closer and farther away than ever before, I lost all notion of my body, all notion of time, staring into that bee-self, the self staring into me, until at last the bees scattered once more, streaming darkly into the air like smoke after an explosion. Then they were gone, the buzzing with them. I staggered up from the grass and ran back to the party, the guests still gossiping, still sipping at their flutes. Did you see that? I asked, but nobody had seen a thing, not a one had looked up.

WHAT WAS THAT

What was that perfection and how to describe it, the car roaring up like something wild let loose from a cage, the door bounding open, that healthy giant emerging with a smile as large as a canyon, the beauty of it a sort of pain, like a passing awe, the sun looking down on us without judgment, and all the air moving with us as we drove through town, the sky like a pure thought, not a cloud in sight, not a cloud even imagined, as if clouds belonged above another sort of earth, not our earth, the earth of that bountiful day, when we fell in love several times an hour with the miracles on the shelves and all the possible selves hanging on the racks, when strangers spoke to us as though we were friends, when strangers blessed us and blessed our food, when we paid for everything we owed and left feeling satisfied, sweets clenched in our fists, when we turned cartwheels and jested like children, as if no wrong had ever been done us and no ugliness ever crossed our lips, and when chords started up from the guitar, crashing through that battered amp, song that sounded like an uprising, loud and strident and brash, I could have died of it, the joy.

AND WHEN I AWOKE

And when I awoke I saw that I was gone. Just like that, the woman I thought I knew, gone into the morning like the mockingbird's song. After all these years it was a bit of a surprise, even though I had seen it coming, the way you see a train approaching from afar, crawling along the tracks, silent at first, and then the chuffing hum, the churning, the wail, plaintive and raw, that pierces the air, the chaos of the train crossing the intersection, holding up traffic, making a terrible noise, the children plugging their ears as the engine grinds by with a muscular, metallic strain, the boxcars grumbling along behind it, and after the train veers at last into the horizon, a trailing quiet; the children unplug their ears, the cars continue on their way and the birds resume their serenade. Yes, that's just what it was like, and still I was surprised. I thought I'd always be here, as if forever, I thought I understood something, but I understood nothing. I left all the same, even though I was still there in the same body, wearing the same clothes, moving in the same gingerly way, saying the same gingerly things, but I was gone, and I was left alone with what was left of me, left to carry on, to carry out whatever was left of the plan, and I wonder to this day where I went, that woman I thought I knew, why I thought I'd ever existed, why I had to leave, why I never came back, why I so loved a leaving.

ACKNOWLEDGMENTS

Profound gratitude to the editors of the journals in which these pieces first appeared:

> *Abstract Magazine TV*: "Because the Sign Was Missing" and "There I Was"
>
> *Antioch Review*: "If Only I Could Take" and "Light a Cigarette"
>
> *Birmingham Poetry Review*: "In the Portrait Gallery" and "On the Brink of This"
>
> *Conduit*: "Sent in the Mail"
>
> *Five Points*: "I Awoke on the Edge"
>
> *Georgia Review*: "I Went Searching," "Martyrs, All of Us," and "When It Hits You"
>
> *Hudson Review*: "Go By, Go By," "Miracle of Mine," and "When I Was Young"
>
> *JMWW*: "We're Marching"
>
> *Lake Effect*: "That Summer"
>
> *Literary Imagination*: "The Exile" and "Nightfall"
>
> *Massachusetts Review*: "But Her Features"
>
> *Narrative*: "The Apocalypse Has Happened" and "What's Happening"
>
> *The Nation*: "They Brought Her In"
>
> *New York Review of Books*: "The Island"
>
> *The Paris Review*: "Here We Are"
>
> *Pembroke Magazine*: "No One Understood" and "What Sounds"
>
> *Ploughshares*: "And When I Awoke"
>
> *Sugar House Review*: "The Jails"
>
> *Tin House*: "The Skull on My Desk"

"Because the Sign Was Missing" is dedicated to Jim Scott and was inspired by visiting his spectacular garden on Lake Martin in Dadeville, Alabama.

"Only Now" was inspired by an exchange with the extraordinary Toi Derricotte.

"What Was That" is dedicated with love and awe to Paris Watel-Young.

THANK YOUS

After decades spent refining your craft, mountains of words, from stories to novels to poems to essays to who-knows-what, the manifold mishaps, the rare triumphs, your entire writing life an enchanted, solitary dream, your entire publishing life a joyless, sweaty slog with little to show for it; after countless rejections—by post, by email, one in a condolence note, one in person; after bouts of despair, bitterness, envy, shame; after nearly forty years of trying, your perseverance sometimes resembling a form of insanity; after all that and more still, when you finally publish a book, at age fifty-seven, you are beyond ecstatic. Even more, you're relieved. Mostly, though, you're grateful.

Throughout my era of torments, everyone kept telling me, "All it takes is one person." Thank you, Ilya Kaminsky, for being that person. I so badly wanted a seat at the table—a stool, a crate, even a stack of pizza boxes would have sufficed—and you pulled out the most elegant, stately chair in the room and asked me to sit. Thank you for giving me this amazing opportunity. I hope I prove worthy of it.

The talented women at Sarabande Books fearlessly ventured into my scary dreamworld to ferry this book into the waking world. Thank you, Kristen Renee Miller, for your incisive editorial smarts and your vision. Thank you, Danika Isdahl, for the sharpest cover on the shelf. Thank you, Joanna Englert and Natalie Wollenzien, for your vigorous advocacy. Thank you, Emma Aprile, for your sensitive edits.

Who would want to take on a book full of cutthroat, deranged, digressive flights of fury and find for this beast a cutthroat, deranged, furious readership? Cassie Mannes Murray, that's who. Thank you, Cassie, for your passion and humanity, your excellence in all endeavors, and your sporting faith in my crazy.

For years I submitted madly. Most journals said no. Sometimes I would get four in a day: no, no, no, no. So thank you, again, to the editors who published potions. With every yes you gave me hope.

Special thanks to Jana Prikryl; your small suggestions improved my work in immense ways.

Thank you, distinguished poets and literary genre busters—Stuart Dybek, Linda Gregerson, Amy Hempel, Garrett Hongo, Ilya Kaminsky, Sabrina Orah Mark, Vijay Seshadri, Tom Sleigh, and Rosanna Warren—who wrote in support of my book. You buoy me with your ingenious work and honor me with your generous words. A deep bow to Garrett, for your very meaningful advocacy at just the right time.

These days, far into middle age, I sometimes glance in the mirror and mistake my reflection for a mask on clearance after Halloween. Thank you, Ashley Kauschinger, for making me look good, like a woman with magic up her sleeves (and down her knickers).

Trying to write without the solidarity of friends is like unwrapping a present that has nothing in it, and the wrapping paper turns into a rotting corpse, which turns into a zombie, and then you have to run, but the door's locked. Thank you to the cherished friends who sustained me on the long winding path to publication: David Alexander, Louanne Bachner, Kelly Beard, Rembert Block, David Bottoms, Kim Boykin, Susan Bridges, Katie Chaple, Scott Daughtridge DeMer, Stephanie Dowda DeMer, Anne Dennington, Travis Denton, Amber Dermont, Greg Fraser, Beth Haas, Sarah Harwell, Arlene Hirsch, Binnie Kirshenbaum, Nicole Livieratos, Alan Loehle, Jenny Lux, Brian Mahan, Jim May, Amy Miller, Chelsea Rathburn, Megan Sexton and Kerry Sherin Wright. You are all gifts beyond measure.

A late bloomer in so many ways, I needed a bountiful, sprawling expanse of soil to grow into my own. From my home turf: Thank you, Rose Watel, for getting us through, for your devilish fun and your fierce devotion. Thank you, Wendy Watel-Burno, for your splendidly dark sense of humor, your sisterly kindness, and your peerless baked goods. Thank you, Jeff Watel, for tolerating my bossy nonsense.

From the garden beyond childhood: Thank you, Jeff Young, darling of a guy and intrepid co-parent; you put the ex- in exceptional, exciting, and exasperating.

Thank you, Amber Boardman, sister wife and co-captain of the USS *Stubborn*; your greatness is damaging, your joy and affection a blessing.

Thank you, Louis Corrigan, for my very life, for your limitless patience and integrity, for your unswerving belief, and for always seeing, and loving, the person I would eventually become, even when I mostly fell short.

Thank you, Edward Hirsch, my love at first remark, husband for the ages, towering literary advocate, adorable goofball, wielder of gladiator charm and monstrous erudition, for showing me what a writer should be: citizen, scholar, perpetual student, impassioned teacher, a lover of craft and servant to the art.

Thank you, Paris Watel-Young, for the wildest, most exhilarating ride of my life. Thank you for your strangeness, your surprising brilliances. Thank you for keeping me decent and fresh. Thank you for our walks and our talks, for knowing the right way. And thank you for all the unearthly, unhinged, hilarious, gorgeous, revelatory moments.

Lauren K. Watel is a poet, fiction writer, essayist, and translator. *Book of Potions,* winner of the Kathryn A. Morton Prize in Poetry from Sarabande Books, is her first book. Her work has appeared widely in journals such as *The Paris Review, New York Review of Books,* and *The Nation.* Her work has also won awards from *Poets & Writers, Writer's Digest,* the *Moment Magazine*-Karma Foundation, and *Mississippi Review.* Her prose poem honoring Justice Ruth Bader Ginsburg was set to music by Pulitzer-winning composer Ellen Taaffe Zwilich, and the piece premiered at the Dallas Symphony Orchestra in 2021. Born and raised in Dallas, Texas, she lives in Decatur, Georgia.

Sarabande Books is a nonprofit independent literary press headquartered in Louisville, Kentucky. Established in 1994 to champion poetry, fiction, and essay, we are committed to creating lasting editions that honor exceptional writing.